Hello Brown Girl

Words from a Brown Woman

Deanne Cunningham

Cover designed by Dee'z Thoughts

This book is a work of fiction. Names, characters, places, and incidents either are products of the author's imagination or are used fictitiously. Any resemblance to actual persons, living or dead, events, or locales is entirely coincidental.

Deanne Cunningham

Printed in the United States of America

Dee'z Thoughts Printing: December 7, 2018

ISBN-9781790946341

This journal is dedicated to my two brown nieces, Jayla and Kailyn. I decided to put words on paper to give them a few words of encouragement. I wanted them to understand that no matter what they are beautiful. I wanted to build their self-esteem by giving them an interactive journal to build their self-esteem, confidence, and let them know that their complexion and hair is magic.
My beautiful Brown Unicorns who are dipped in honey.

Hello Brown Girl,
You are beautiful! Never let
anyone tell you any different.

Write down three positive things about yourself.

_____

_____

_____

_____

_____

_____

_____

_____

_____

_____

_____

_____

_____

_____

Hello Brown Girl,
The world may try to dull your shine but remember you were made to sparkle in spite of other people's insecurities that they try to project on you.

How do you show yourself love?

_____

_____

_____

_____

_____

_____

_____

_____

Hello Brown Girl,
Don't let your crown droop, you are a Queen in training. (This means that no matter what is going on around you be sure to keep your head held high.)

What are some ways that you deal with feeling overwhelmed?

_____

_____

_____

_____

_____

_____

_____

_____

Hello Brown Girl,
Your skin is beautiful, no matter the shade. You will often be imitated but never duplicated. That melanin is what others crave to have but you were blessed to be born with it.

When you look in the mirror, what do you see?

_____

_____

_____

_____

_____

_____

_____

Hello Brown Girl,
There will be people that will tell you that you cannot do what others can do. Don't get mad! Just show up, show out, and prove them wrong.

Write about your goals for the next year.

_____

_____

_____

_____

_____

_____

_____

_____

Hello Brown Girl,
You were born to succeed.

What do you want to succeed at? (School, sports, etc.)

_____

_____

_____

_____

_____

_____

_____

_____

_____

_____

_____

_____

_____

_____

Hello Brown Girl,
Do what makes you happy.

What are some things that make you happy?

_____

_____

_____

_____

_____

_____

_____

_____

_____

_____

_____

_____

_____

Hello Brown Girl,
You are smart! You are
beautiful! Be kind! You can do
anything you set your mind to.

Say the above line to yourself. What do you define beauty as?

_____

_____

_____

_____

_____

_____

_____

_____

_____

_____

_____

_____

Hello Brown Girl,
Confidence is the best thing you
can have. Rock it like your life
depends on it.

How do you let your confidence shine?

_____

_____

_____

_____

_____

_____

_____

_____

_____

_____

_____

Hello Brown Girl,
Don't be afraid to step outside of your box. Be whatever your heart desires — if it's a doctor, lawyer, a judge, etc.♥

I am good at.......

_____

_____

_____

_____

_____

_____

_____

_____

_____

_____

Hello Brown Girl, You are enough! Say, "I am enough, I am worthy, and I am beautiful."

Look in the mirror and say 3 positive things about yourself. Then write them below.

_____

_____

_____

_____

_____

_____

_____

_____

_____

_____

_____

Hello Brown Girl,
Everyone will not be happy to see
you succeed in this life but keep
going. Their unhappiness doesn't
affect your shine.

I am proud of me because......

_____

_____

_____

_____

_____

_____

_____

_____

_____

Hello Brown Girl,
Work hard for the things that you want in this life. Nothing is handed to you.

MIRROR TIME: Look directly in your eyes and say, "I will succeed."

_____

_____

_____

_____

_____

_____

_____

_____

_____

_____

_____

Hello Brown Girl,
Make sure you surround yourself
with people who have similar
dreams, aspirations, and work ethic
as you. The saying goes,
"Birds of a feather flock
together."

Do your friends work as hard as you to achieve their goals? (Important because you want like-minded individuals around you).

_____

_____

_____

_____

_____

_____

_____

_____

Hello Brown Girl,
Don't put any limits on yourself
because the world already does that
for you.

Write down 5 positive things you can do.

_____

_____

_____

_____

_____

_____

_____

_____

_____

_____

_____

Hello Brown Girl,
There will be times when you feel treated unfairly because of the color your skin. Don't let that discourage you from being all that you can be.

Write down 3 positive things that no one knows about you.

_____

_____

_____

_____

_____

_____

_____

_____

_____

*Hello Brown Girl,
Stop comparing yourself to others. We were never meant to be like the next person. You are unique!*

What are a couple of things that you like about your body?

_____

_____

_____

_____

_____

_____

_____

_____

_____

Hello Brown Girl,
Society will try to tear you down in every way possible. Stand strong in your sparkles and keep shining because you are a

BROWN UNICORN.

Be like Poppy and keep sparkling. What makes you standout in a crowd?

_____

_____

_____

_____

_____

_____

_____

_____

_____

_____

Hello Brown Girl,
Kinky hair is beautiful.
Curly hair is beautiful.
Straight hair is beautiful.
You are beautiful.

What do you like about your hair?

_____

_____

_____

_____

_____

_____

_____

_____

_____

_____

Hello Brown Girl,
Hold your head up always.
Remember confidence is key.
No one is better than you and
never treat others like they are
beneath you.

MIRROR TIME: Say, "I am just as smart, beautiful, and worthy as anyone else."
Write down how you feel after repeating those words.

_____

_____

_____

_____

_____

_____

_____

_____

Hello Brown Girl,
You were not made to be like
others, you were born to stand out
in the crowd. You are a rare gem.

What makes you different from those around you?

_____

_____

_____

_____

_____

_____

_____

_____

_____

_____

_____

_____

Hello Brown Girl,

Your skin is as smooth as milk chocolate, your heart is as pure as gold, and your hair is simply beautiful.

MIRROR TIME: Take time and admire everything beautiful about you. Write it down.

_____

_____

_____

_____

_____

_____

_____

_____

_____

_____

Hello Brown Girl,
Light skin is beautiful.
Mocha skin is beautiful.
Chocolate skin is beautiful.
All shades are beautiful.
Melanin Rainbows are
beautiful.

What do you like about your complexion? Remember this is a negative free zone and if you have any negative thoughts push them to the side.

_____

_____

_____

_____

_____

_____

_____

_____

Hello Brown Girl,
Your hair is your crown and glory.

MIRROR TIME: My hair is beautiful and I am beautiful. Say that each and every day to yourself. Write down all the positive thoughts you had after saying those words.

_____

_____

_____

_____

_____

_____

_____

_____

_____

_____

_____

_____

_____

_____

_____

Hello Brown Girl,
Use your voice. Your voice is just as important as your counterparts.

Scream at the top of your lungs and say, "I AM IMPORTANT." How did you feel after screaming that at the top of your lungs?

_____

_____

_____

_____

_____

_____

_____

_____

_____

_____

_____

_____

Hello Brown Girl,
It is okay to be different because you are black magic. Super powerful and rare, so embrace all that makes you different.

What does black magic mean to you?

_____

_____

_____

_____

_____

_____

_____

_____

_____

_____

_____

Hello Brown Girl,
Say this, "My Brownness is excellent, my Brownness is enough, my Brownness is important, and my Brownness is magic."

MIRROR TIME: Repeat the above words three times with a smile. Write down how your brownness is excellent.

_____

_____

_____

_____

_____

_____

_____

_____

Hello Brown Girl,
Don't define your brownness
according to the standards of the
world.

What standards do you measure yourself by? (Hint: Your standards are the only standards that matter).

_____

_____

_____

_____

_____

_____

_____

_____

_____

_____

_____

_____

Hello Brown Girl,
Love everything that makes you,
you – from your lips to your nose
to your hair (that can be hard to
deal with at times) to your wide
hips to the color of your skin.

What's your favorite thing about yourself?

_____

_____

_____

_____

_____

_____

_____

_____

Hello Brown Girl,
You have to love you first before you ever expect someone else to love you.

How do you show yourself love?

_____

_____

_____

_____

_____

_____

_____

_____

_____

_____

_____

_____

Hello Brown Girl,

I pray that all your dreams come true, from the smallest dream to the most gigantic one of all. I pray you succeed in this life, because life will get hard and there will be times you will want to give up. I pray that you won't though. I pray that you push harder when things seem to not go as planned. My overall prayer is that you find your way in this life.

Love Always,

Deanne Cunningham
A Brown Woman

Deanne Cunningham

Extra Journal Pages

Use these pages to write down all of the positive things that are occurring in your life.

_____

_____

_____

_____

_____

_____

_____

_____

_____

_____

_____

_____

_____

_____

_____

_____

_____

_____

_____

_____

_____

_____

_____

_____

_____

_____

_____

_____

_____

_____

_____

_____

_____

_____

_____

_____

_____

_____

_____

_____

_____

_____

_____

_____

_____

_____

_____

_____

_____

_____

_____

_____

_____

_____

_____

_____

_____

_____

_____

_____

_____

_____

_____

_____

_____